Praise

Cameron's writing has a way of wrapping you up in quiet comfort, insisting you pay attention to the little things that make life.

– Rebecca Gunn

Author of *This is the Descent*

Cameron takes us on a journey through her life as a rural daughter, a wife, a mother, a friend, and a teacher. At times an emotional gut punch, and other times, smile-inducing, it is a deeply personal work of nostalgia and stripped-to-the-bone emotion, with an occasional turn and a hint of sharp humor.

– Rosalie Spielman

Author of the award winning *Hometown Mysteries*

With vivid word-pictures, Cherice Cameron paints a multifaceted look into life experiences. The highs and the lows show the beauty of her world taking the reader right into the moment.

– Lieutenant Colonel Charlene Purtee

United States Air Force

Cameron's poetry reflects a life rich with exploration-covering every aspect-written with clear prose & multifaceted creativity.

– Crystal Reyes

Author of *Wildflower Blooming*

Cherice Cameron's keen observations and intimate portraits of both nature and family has the reader feeling she knows these people, she has seen this flower. Each poem is a small gift to savor.

– Margaret Elysia Garcia

Author of *The Daughterland*

Cherice Cameron's poems are raw and real. She takes the reader on a journey of love, laughter, joy, pain, resilience, struggle, but above all this book highlights hope. A strength of spirit that we can all be inspired by.

– Erica Castro

Author of *Creating Peace Through the Grieving Process*

Gamut Eclectic & Mundane

Life Perspectives

Cherice Cameron

Gamut Eclectic & Mundane:
Life Perspectives

Foreword by: Lynn Dean Cameron

Cherice Cameron

Gamut Eclectic & Mundane: Life Perspectives
© 2024 Cherice Cameron
ISBN: 979-8-9900531-8-2
Library of Congress control number: 2024918719

Cover art © 2024, Lynn Michael Ramsey
Illustrations © 2024, Lynn Michael Ramsey and Beatrice Sofia Falcone
Photography © 2024, Lynn D. Cameron, Cameron Artworks

First Edition, 2024

Printed in the United States of America

Edited by Kimiko White
Cover & Layout Design by Jolene Garrettson

Dedicated to

Marsha Ann Folks

(1950 - 2012)

as promised in 1983

Foreword

I was there when Cherice took her first breath. Her mother and I walk with her through a life that runs the gamut from the sublime to the horrific, an eclectic kaleidoscope of significant and mundane experiences from which she formed her personal perspectives and gained the wisdom she shares through her poetry. Reading it is an adventure into a multifaceted world that intrigues, informs, and catalyzes change. I have grown as a person by reading and rereading her writing.

Cherice wrote her first poem at age three. It is no surprise that "in the beginning," speaks in the voice of a newborn, of her own birth experience and of the ultimate importance of her mother. In "pieced together," multi-generational love, sacrifice, gratitude, belonging, safety, warmth, calm, and self-identity are woven into a beautiful picture of a child being tucked into bed under a hand sewn patchwork quilt.

That sublime image is offset by "raw," which expresses the horror of spousal abuse experiences, exposes them for what they are, shows the pattern they followed, and courageously brings them into open view. For her and her family that exposure made a safe house possible, secured legal, medical and emotional assistance and broke the cycle of abuse. If this book helps do the same for even one person or family, it will be a great service.

"photos on the farm," describes me, the family photographer, who created slideshows set to music. I didn't fully understand what the shows meant to me until I read Cherice's poem. "'I knew that every slide and every note spoke his soul to the world, shouting 'Listen!' 'These are the people that I love!'"

Love of Nature flows through her carefully chosen words. "hymntide," speaks of being consumed in Nature when "...a full moon reached into my soul and took all of me..." She finds kinship with fellow travelers on Earth. "To the Egg Sack Carrying Spider on My Patio," explores her desire to commune with a spider. Hmmmm?

She knows loss. In "trees" she explores mourning so deeply over the death of a close friend that she could not speak of. In "Still," she laments the criminal homicide of an innocent friend and marvels at the profound lesson in forgiveness that grew out of the tragedy. "these knees" outlines the unspoken trust she had in the ability of her body until injury and pain raised unanswered questions.

Cherice maintains a life-long sense of humor. It is illustrated by the titles, "Netflix Instant Streaming And The Day I Shot The Television: A Tall Tale (or Not)," and "Just Another Stupid White Woman (Perspective from a state of disbelief: i.e., people are rude)." I predict that you will laugh when you read and reread these poems. I did!

She loves cats, dogs and other small animals. They respond in kind to her. "A Blind Deaf Crooked Dog in an Aardvark World," details the depth of her love and care for her disabled dog. The poem acknowledges that she will outlive her dear friend and mourn his passing. A memorial service for two beloved dogs eases grief and brings peace in "Angel of the Waters."

At age four Cherice wrote in red crayon across the front of a new unfinished set of dresser drawers. Oh yes, twice! Writing is an imperative of her life. She is schooled in *Creative Writing* and *English Literature*. She sometimes goes on a lunch date with a book of poetry. See "lunch: with poets." "I used to love to write," is a narrative of how for a time, as an adult, she lost her ability to read. How can that be?

Our home was welcoming to foreign visitors and exchange students. They were treated as family for a meal, a weekend or several months. That experience and Cherice's travels, attendance and work in schools from kindergarten to university, exposed her to thousands of diverse individuals and groups. She developed the sense of justice, compassion, love, and kinship that is evident in "While Sunflowers Fight to Stand in Fields of Blood: Ukrainian Mothers Love Their Babies Too." The same is true of "abide with me," and "skull cricket," written for Native children who died in boarding schools and for their families. After reading "Rebellion," about a bullied student, I resolved to ALWAYS stand with youth who are being mistreated and be vocal in opposing exclusionary actions.

Cherice likes puzzles. It is no surprise to find a few in her book. I was so puzzled by "These Cathedral Halls Have Flowers as Ears," that I went to the internet to find a basis for understanding it. I called Cherice about "Reconciliation," an art response poem, and learned it is about a Nkisi Nkondi sculpture in NYC by an anonyomous African artist in the Congo. This figure traditionally has been used to reconcile disputes. "riding its back—a riddle—," is just that. Good luck!

Cherice Cameron's approach to life is to maintain a broad world view and move ahead and grow no matter what challenges events present, to discover the necessary change in herself, and leave others whole in the process. In "solitary redemption," she describes how to make intergenerational change and emerge more beautiful than before, as in the Japanese Kintsugi method of repairing broken pottery using lacquer mixed with gold, silver or platinum.

I have read, reread and analyzed the messages from this collection of poetry. It is like a compact reference book on living life. I wholeheartedly recommend it to you and those you care about.

Lynn D. Cameron
Writer/Photographer/Storyteller

Table of Contents

Acknowledgments

To my students who have seen me at my best and worst, your gifts of art, stories, plays, poems, compositions, and of friendship are inspiring to me. You amaze me with your kindness, growth, perseverance, creativity, and enthusiasm for life. Thank you for allowing me to walk with you in discovery and learning, and for reminding me that stories are to be shared.

To all of those who have traveled this life gamut with me, thank you for sharing your expertise, your perspectives, and for walking with me in discovery and life experience.

Thank you to: Allie Pfeiffer and Bill Fey, my COVID era writer's circle, and to my Community Literature Initiative peers who walked with me to the finish line. Hiram Sims for creating CLI, a gathering of poets and goldmine of human creativity. Margaret Garcia, ever patient and brilliant for acting as our beacon on this journey. Crystal Reyes for her enthusiasm and undying support. Rebecca Chaffee, my accountability partner and my "just a text away" rock of support. Kimiko White and Jolene Garrettson for being fabulous people and editors. Erica Castro, my amazing publisher, for believing in me.

To my mentors, teachers, and professors for providing places of learning and growth. Marsha Folks, you knew before I did that this book would be a reality. Ron McFarland, even when things were unraveling in nearly every aspect of my life you gave me a chance to get up again and keep trying to reach my educational and writing goals. Thank you.

To my family and friends who always saw what I did not. First and foremost Lynn and Susan Cameron, my parents, my foundation, my dream makers and my inspiration. You are my beginning and you are my everything. Margaret Suhr, you are my person and fellow discoverer, thank you for the beauty, the music, and for your poetry mail. Julie Pierce, thank you for being my sounding board and confidant.

To my sisters and their spouses: Kristin & Brent Huddleston, Kara
& Daniel Poppleton, Kisha Cameron, Kayce & Miguel Ramirez,
and McKenzie Cameron. You are all part of this book and future
publications. Thank you for sharing this life with me and for your
AMAZING families whom I adore. This book would not be what it is
without you!

To my niblings: Soraya & Steven Zinn and baby Eloise, Joshua, Ryan,
and Darren Huddleston, Sean, Braden, Seth, and Jocelyn Poppleton,
Johan Boll, Rachel & Alice Bayly, Oscar, Silas, and Aquira Ramirez,
Kelanie, Tavi & Serik Cameron-Sandi. Thank you for being the
creative, motivated, talented, amazing human beings that you are.

To my amazing blended family, children, and grandchildren: Jefferson
Ramsey & Stacie Flores and "Baby" Genevieve, Nick and Artemis
Cassleman, McKay MacArach, Lynn Michael Ramsey & Bea Falcone,
Joseph Ramsey & Teresa Moote Ramsey, Emilia & Jonathan Weaver
and baby Athena, Olivia Ramsey Rolirad, Eunice Dundas & "the
boys" Mikhail, Rylan, and Chance, Samantha Babb and her Jax.
Jeffrey & Anne Ramsey, Wiola & Allan Stott, Ulises Cedeño, Daniel
Christiansen, Jamie Babb. We have traveled a long way together
through challenges and triumphs, love and loss, sorrow, happiness,
and joy and I can't imagine it without you.

To my friends who have supported me in good times and bad: Pamela
Jean Houser, Dani Villaflor Elbeshlawy, Charlene Purtee, Kathy
Therianos, Nikki Crathorne & Jordan Abendroth, Angie Sharp,
Stanley Hawks, and Tina Smith & Angel Buscaglia.

Additionally, I want to thank Jefferson for memorizing my favorite
poem, Lunar Baedeker (Mina Loy) with me on our drive and for
undying encouragement. McKay for "fifty-seven minutes" to Brooklyn,
NYC walks and musicals. You followed your dreams while supporting
me in mine. Lynn Michael for being my amazing cover artist, support,
and for the inspiration of your art and music. Joseph for creating
and selling your beautiful woodwork in order to help support my CLI
experience and for refusing to let me quit writing this book. Emilia,
Olivia, and Wiola for your continual encouragement and support.

Preface

I tell my students that the most fair thing about life is that life is not fair. It is the truth. I find that when I recognize that the unexpected is as fair as the mundane, it is easier to refocus my gaze and find a new way of living within a moment. Bad things happen and sometimes good things come from them and the opposite is also true. So I ask: How can we, as human beings, walk through each day and find a path, through the gamut of life that builds rather than destroys?

Treat each other with kindness and recognize that a moment barefoot in the grass, or sand, or water, or mud, can reset perspective. So can an event of sorrow, pain, joy, shock, delight, or mundanity. It is okay to settle into these experiences long enough to discover a new path, long enough to heal, to grow, to move forward and wayfind in the day to day. Settle in a while and know that you, human being, body of cells, holder of memories, are who you are and you are glorious.

Gamut Eclectic & Mundane:
Life Perspectives

Hell's Canyon Road in Winter by Lynn D. Cameron

in the beginning

in the beginning there was light
& my mother never made a sound

a tiny lady
she resonated as i moved her bones

pushed them out of my way
elongated head playing peek-a-boo

nearly born i
womb swaddled

rode as she worked
& emerged

to breast curve
& elbow crook

her eyes – suns of my existence
her face the firmament

safety

olive drab & taut
held by rock-struck stakes
temporary family home

she wore an orange hat
big white polka dots
wide brim

his pockets full
necessary things
pocket knife, string

& baby me
secure between
he & she

first visit

Granddad bought me
lunch in the hospital cafe
& a pink-eared bunny with
a baby face
as i waited to meet you

people paused to peek
and coo—
swaddled in a window box
you rivaled the best
department store display

a strange first introduction
—i lifted up
you—on display in a
hospital wall

my eyes kissed your
pinkness
& memorized your
newness

no window box could stop
that love

milk & daughters

i was not allowed
  in the milk barn
grandpa let me
  peek in the door
a dim room & men on stools
  i loved those men

once grandpa told my mother
  no daughter of mine will
ever milk a cow
  i soon learned that i
was also a daughter
  no milking for me

when those cans were full
  i jumped in grandpa's truck
& we drove to town
  i watched for the corner
where we turned to deliver milk
  for porch jugs & cheese

sometimes grandpa took me
  along with uncles
who made me giggle & smile
  as we bumped along
country roads to auction

fifty dollar bid now sixty
  will ya give me sixty
sixty dollar bid now seventy
  will ya give me seventy

folks bought one calf after another
  to a farm girl's lullaby

gully garden after heavy rain

nineteen seventy-five
sunny & a touch of cloud

two neighbor boys
dressed for a funeral

& three little girls
six, two

& a baby
waist deep in goopy ground

three muddy girls &
two slick-haired boys

mourning an old man
& clean white button-ups

mourning an old man
& a day without mud

The Summer My Mother Buried Our Second Dog

Grandpa woke early to milk cows
Left for town in a truck full of milk jugs
Before my eyes had opened to breeze and yawn

Lace curtains blew inward
Lifted up like a hoop skirt at a ladies quick turn
Long enough for my little head to peek

Across the grass
Past the paddock fence

To my mother with her heel on a shovel
Stomp and toss
Stomp and toss

pieced together

tuck me in under quilts sewn by
mothers & grandmothers & aunts

tiny
even
stitches

pin-pricked fingers sucked clean
by lips of women with needles

thousands of
blood reminders

pull up the covers &
tuck the edges tight

sing me to sleep
sing songs in sing song

tuck me in under cotton
expressions of love
& sacrifice
& womb warmth
& calm

hold my face in your hands
kiss my forehead

trace the fabric from
your first-grade dress
from grandpa's flannel shirt
trace you in my face
& tuck me in tight

Between the Lines

Between the lines are places
villages full of cat-headed cowboys
and self-baking fruit pies
crisp white sheets and silk pillowcases full
of the moment between sleep and dreams
crisp white sheets tucked tight
lullaby and hum

Between the lines are places
grassy places
warm places with a breeze
bumblebees plump and buzz
mossy resting places
between daydream and song
soft pillows to rest upon

Between the lines are places
symphony hall pin drop
sound carried to recessed chandeliers
collectors of dust and stories
stories and song
between crystal reflections
stories told between crisp white sheets

Photos on the Farm

My father, the official family photographer, capturer of memories
became our historian in kodachrome an artist at work and at play
His photographs were the final feature of every epic holiday

Epic is an understatement when you consider an Idaho
farm complete with cows, chickens, hay stacks, and enough raspberries
To eat all day long and still have buckets full to take in to grandma

My father created a slideshow complete with music, handpicked perfection –
We cheered, kids and adults alike
each time the slide changed
"It's me!" "It's you" "Look!" "Look!"

I knew every song by heart because he was my dad and I
his firstborn girl was invested in his creation
I knew that every slide and every note
spoke his soul to the world, shouting "Listen!"
"These are the people that I love!"

An Acre of Flowers

Church was beautiful the moment my grandma arrived
She let me carry her flowers up the stairs to the pulpit
A spiritual journey for a little girl in charge of God's creation

She had an acre of flowers fed with ditch water
I see her bent down with a hoe in her hand
A moment of cloud over the earth she cleared
A cool breeze to the microcosm around her feet

I imagine her bent over munitions during the war
She did her part to bring our men home alive
A single seam drawn up the back of her leg
Was the line of a woman who accepted sacrifice

Her voice resonated through my body as she sang her favorite hymn
Onward Christian soldiers marching on to war with the cross of...
Church was beautiful the moment my grandma arrived

Literary Farming

Poetry eat me like mashed potatoes & gravy on an Idaho farm

Feed me to form and rhyme
Let me digest a while in metaphor
Wading squishy in stomach lining
Barefoot & pregnant with words

Color haiku in hues found in fairy tales & fairy circles

Let pollywogs swim in ditch water that
Flows to beet-stained blades of combines &
Fingers of farmers whose wives can cucumbers in brine & dill
For winter crunch on sandwiches of scripture & egg

Tunnel through apples with worms who sit & eat around sweet rooms

Myth and hope for five seeds—
Proof of God's word in dusty Bibles
As children giggle & dance
Amongst sinners whose sweat sticks to dusty brows

Write soliloquies on the pods of peas shucked on homestead stairs

Love songs saved for baby's breath
Allegories of ants and grasshoppers
Stories from a grandmother's lips whose fingers never stop
As she takes a breath to begin again

letters of Scotland

she mails poetry
writes of snow &
a granddad in Scotland

a highland stream—
fly rod air pulled
with a flick

she sends discovery
on paper
speaks word music

I need her misty breath
stories of home—
long distance heart-to-heart

Dedicated to Margaret Suhr

trees

speak for me
& mourn

this blue day—

as
petals
drift
into
a
six
foot
deep
hole

&
hand
full
s
of
d
i
r
t

flit
across a coffin lid

ashes
to
ashes

while
she
&
her unborn
baby

its tiny hands
curled
beneath
her skin

become
soil
beneath

toes
in grass
beneath

tiny weeds
with purple
blossoms

sway
   in
the
   wind

   &
weep
with
me

Dedicated to Pamela Jean Bone Houser & her unborn baby

hymntide

hymns came rolling in
on high tide

a full moon–

reached into my soul &
took all of me

on smooth waves
to a sea of fishes

one note, two
three notes, four

those chords
carried me &

kept watch until dawn
& the morning star

A Blind Deaf Crooked Dog in an Aardvark World

Oh dog, your tilted head and lolling tongue
Your blinded eyes and lack of working ears
At sixteen years your life is nearly done
Each day a gift among the passing years

Our daily ritual stretch and yawn become
A rhythm, song, a poem of the morn
I stroke your back and ears and you succumb
A yawn, a stretch, sweet dog, you keep me warm

But when you choose to leave this mortal place
Alone I'll be to ponder empty rooms
Your scent, a blanket, toy, an empty space
All memories of us upon a loom

Oh Happy dog, my friend you'll always be
A gift from God, a precious memory

reverse window washer

moist terra sniffer
you leave spots on my window
canine auto companion

last breath

room quiet
I tuck you in one last time
dance in the meadow

undisturbed
a poof of your fur
I remember your first day

sunbeam nap beam
breath among angels
even the dust motes miss you

whirligig

i want to
lift the lid
from your urn

i want to
dance in ash–
you once more

i want to
watch a wind
take you home

Angel of the Waters

I said goodbye at the feet of an
angel in Central Park
Our parting well attended

A decade and a half released to
songbirds and passing dogs

Cherubim and chubby squirrels
read soliloquies in chorus
Dissonance begged resolve

A decade and a half carried on
the wind by artists in the park

Wings of angels
Wings of birds
Wings of song

A decade and a half carried on
the wind by artists in the park

Dissonance begged resolve
Cherubim and chubby squirrels
read soliloquies in chorus

A decade and a half released to
songbirds and passing dogs

Our parting well attended
I said goodbye at the feet of an
angel in Central Park

Bethesda Fountain, NYC

duet

i   ii

blue dogs   onyx eyes
sing with the sun   ride canine

chase   a silver band
stars &   gaseous mass
moons
& planets   cats whine
                         moon song
strut
around Saturn   altar cry
                         of the stars

nap
crater curled

dream moon side
breathe earth tide

ethereal jewelry
A nod to Mina Loy

black tourmaline
hugs a silver band
while cats whine
their moon song

a cry to the altar of the stars
a ring on my finger
a curio
a curiosity
a felted mat of fur
a coat

& in my dreams
two blue dogs dance
a cat cry waltz

leap from star to star
follow a space trail

of stellectric soot
in a floral sky

thunderhead

one more poem
for the road
where hawks play

as pavement
turns into
loose gravel

skies tempt rain
while words soar
on raptor wings

Slate Creek Crooner

snow in june
& a scarlet breasted finch
sings a new song

a birdsong flirt

a five branch
tango for two & an observer

& a river breeze
& a trout eddy
& a carpet of wildflowers

he sings
puff breasted
& waits

water burial

mosquito
bits are for
killing gnats–

seem harmless
seem to like
to die in

the bathtub–
convenient
cemetery

centrifugal force

time compressed sand
stone on stone
held fast

when i am with you

when i am with you
eddies are your eyes

a current embrace—

 your arms
pull me close

& i float

riding its back
—a riddle—

speak from the altar
of sand polished shards &
moldered bone
where western wine runs
red as blood –
clotting agent of the horse
& the tortoise –
rabid molasses
devil's purse unhatched –

killer unborn
two hundred and fourteen
pounds of cartilaginous beauty
roulette & nature

i dip a toe & dive
to meet what was born
speak of the devil

quarterback

he caught the long pass
audible crack and crumple
a touchdown to death

i thawed a crocodile

frozen solid
i was begged to save it

chip
      chip
            chip
                 away the ice

heat its skin with mine

palm on face
palm on back
palm
running
down
the
length
of
its
spine
     until
          it breathes
                again

i was asked to save a crocodile

while locked
in
its jaws

abduction

scream of a bunny
teeth of a cat
a desire to change
something i can't

Road to Somewhere

I rode the ribbon home after you died
Each line began again after it stopped
I cried as I remembered years of lies
Memories of you both bold and cropped

Each line began again after it stopped
Blue veins drained red the day you left
Memories of you both bold and cropped
A weight of time, a toll, a weave and weft

Blue veins drained red the day you left
Machine ground bones pour from an urn
A weight of time, a toll, a weave and weft
A night, a day, a year, a lifetime spurn

Machine ground bones pour from an urn
A pile of dust and my heart stopped
A night, a day, a year, a lifetime spurn
I rode a ribbon home after you died

another time

the night you put your head
through the bedroom
door

is marked with a hole
the size of your forehead

wide and jagged

a calendar
a journal entry
a timeline hash

it is still there

a gaping mouth
with nothing left to say

raw

the day he put his head through the door
was not the same day
he tried to put his head
through the mirror

it was not the day he screamed in my face
until I passed out

it was not the day he gave me roses

it was not the day
he brought me a new puppy

it feels like the same day
it feels like yesterday
& a century ago

my cheek still aches
where his hand met my face

my eyes do not focus anymore

the one I loved most hit me the hardest
reached into my chest
grabbed my heart
& ripped it
from between
my ribs

blood
drips
from his
chin

& the bite he took
was big enough
to gag us
both

battleskars

i cannot—

rub away
print of hand
on this cheek

mend
hamburger skin
in this mouth

replicate
sturdiness
of this jaw

&
the
door
asks
through
splintered
mahogany

why did he hit you—

put his fist
where it did not
belong?

i answer—

love
inquires
of the devil

a cheater
& a liar

as though he
has the answers

lock and key

plain white wall
will i stay
will i go

indecision
yet one nail
begets another

commitment
in your art
on my walls

ampersand

i hear your breath
as i turn to board

embrace the space between us
breathe slow & walk away
you become a dream life

my gaze & your art
pain & paint & a longing
for home

you & me on opposite trains
destination unknown

Painted

I will paint it white
Cover all of my sins

Another coat
& another

I will glue
Torn corners of wicked wallpaper
Whitewash every surface clean

I will renew old clothes
Take in seams
Stretched by anger & pain

Fill cavities in my soul
With fiberfill & charity

& stitch tears with blood
Red is the blood of grace
Blue is the blood of royalty
White is the cloth of repentance

Netflix Instant Streaming And The Day I Shot the Television: A Tall Tale (or Not)

I don't know what happened
and I'm given to lying
from time to time.

Like yesterday
when I told my husband
what happened to the television
in the basement

What I do know
is that I took a long, hot, bath
after I shot that thing,
and spooned
ice cream
into my mouth
by candlelight.

Oh, Garlic!

Roasted, toasted, slathered
on my morning bagel
Oh Garlic, you are so regal

Buttered, minced, sauteed
tossed in angel hair
Oh Garlic, you are so dear

Skinned, chopped, blended
chickpea delight
Oh Garlic you are hummus tonight

11k molar

17 years
s-e-v-e-n-t-e-e-n years
and one of the teeth loosed by a hand
is going to cost
another F-O-U-R thousand dollars

yes i spelled it out

i will have an 11k tooth in my head if it survives this trip
to the endodontist

an insult to injury after
root canals
& injections that smell like bleach

a singing dentist
pushed a plunger to save my teeth

i need this tooth

it is my package opening tooth
it holds string I need taut
it is part of a four-year smile

now it is a cap over a festering jaw-hole
& each tag I remove is a slow step in a funeral procession
for an old friend

Teeth Are Reliable Tools

Everyday, top drawer utensils, teeth
Nothing better for cutting newborn nails

Teeth put clippers to shame

Break a seal–
        satisfaction

Rip crusty bread–
        great with cheese

Enamel against horsehair–
        nuisance free
                bow against string

And

In the Art of Loving
        a well placed nibble
                        —sigh

Teeth are reliable tools

To the Egg Sac Carrying Spider on My Patio

You intrigue me little lady
Carry your silken sac across bricks and gravel
Let us commune amongst flowers
Share your secrets to egg-carrying
Tell me stories while you labor

&

Sit in the moonlight

We sisters &

I will honor you

&

Tell you stories while you labor
Share your secrets to egg-carrying
Let us commune amongst flowers
Carry your silken sac across bricks and gravel
You intrigue me little lady

While Sunflowers Fight to Stand in Fields of Blood:
Ukrainian Mothers Love Their Babies Too

I sit in an atrium of ancient stone
With a Central Park view

While mothers push babies on swings
While trees sing & dance a wind waltz

I breathe in solitude among strangers

I read a parent's plea via forwarded email

"...everyone who can hold a weapon
has risen to defend the capital
even pensioners, students, and
school children"

I stare at ancient walls
Rebuilt stone by stone under glass

While mothers sing songs to their babies under bomb crushed streets

While sunflowers fight to stand in fields of blood

While a grandmother poisons pies to save lives

The writing is on the walls

bee

i sat at a worn coffee shop table
& a bee joined me

she rested on my arm long enough
to exchange a morning greeting

a moment of grateful respite –
her a foothold

& i
a glance at her beauty

Drawing by Beatrice Sofia Falcone

still

i danced with him
talked with him
considered him a friend
though a different sum
equaled this friendship

mathematically brilliant
—socially awkward
he was smarter than all of us
kinder—

he walked a path
we didn't take time to see

even i whispered behind his back a few times
i felt regret
feel regret
regret is uncomfortable

even more uncomfortable—
visiting his grave
knowing that in his kindness
his trust
yes
innocence

they took him out
and shot him in
the back
of the
head
for his car and a couple grand

the world is not a better place
without him

it is better
because his mother
forgave them

killing her oldest son

it is better
because she forgave
anyone

who had ever
wronged her

i know because she told me

she could not forgive
those men
if she held lesser grudges

some lessons are learned the hard way

some grave markers are more than they appear

abide with me

I

one by one
individual petals drop

remedies of a holistic nature
(and remedies of spite)

graves sing earth song chants
of lost children without redress
met on roads of dust and tears

moths drown
kiddie pool grave in blue plastic

seekers float

fire seekers burn

fallen architecture
&
cheap death

someone's child
among photographs & jewelry

abode of the lost
earth grave

earth mother

II

Despite google search
Insipid petals

Ancestral wounds,
Gutteral mourning,

Night water–
One way out or another

& Someone's family
& Eventide

Sing grave songs
& lullabies

III

one by one
individual petals drop
despite google search remedies
of a holistic nature (and remedies of spite)

insipid petals
graves sing earth song chants of lost children
ancestral wounds
without redress

met on roads of dust and tears
guttural mourning

moths drown
kiddie pool grave in blue plastic
night water seekers float
fire seekers burn

one way out or another

fallen architecture &
cheap death &

Someone's family
& someone's child
amongst photographs
& jewelry

eventide
abode of the lost earth grave
earth mother
sing grave songs & lullabies

IV

individual petals drop   one   by   one Despite google search
remedies of a holistic nature (and remedies of spite) Insipid petals.

graves sing earth song chants of lost children   Ancestral wounds
without redress met on roads of dust and tears   Guttural mourning.

moths drown   kiddie pool grave in blue plastic   Night water
seekers float   fire seekers burn   One way out or another.

fallen architecture & cheap cheap cheap death & Someone's family &
someone's child amongst photographs & jewelry   Eventide

abode of the lost   earth grave   Earth Mother   Sing grave songs &
lullabies

"abide with me" and "skull cricket" are dedicated to the children, found and returned to their ancestral lands, and to those yet to be found. May their spirits find peace, their stories be heard, and their legacies honored."

skull cricket

child of the ground, child of the earth
receive your name, Native & crossed
beneath the rock, your name rebirth
hosts of skull hill declared you lost

return to ancient valley-fields
your name spoken, your name sealed
no rock, no sand, not cross-nail bound
child of the earth, child of the ground

REBELLION!
2024 & No Child Should Die Like This

i do not concur
i do not concur
i DO not concur

do you hear me
do YOU hear me
do you HEAR ME

You—who hate
instead of LOVE—

Nex Benedict is dead

did you see Them
in the photo
with Their kitten

They just
They only
They walked

into a bathroom
to pee
like we all do

They trusted
like we all do
in we the PEOPLE

in we the people
They trusted
in we the people

when They were ALIVE!

Nkisi Nkondi

I

fill my head with seeds
& seal it up

fill my belly with ashes
& wasp stingers

give me a mirror navel

give me a nail to the eye

lick metal shards
& pound them deep

again
&
again
&
again

give me deep pocked skin

give me iron fingers

& let me grab a passerby
fill my nostrils with spilled coffee

& let me grab another
fill my casket with grass

II

fill my casket with grass
fill my head with seeds

& seal it up
& let me grab another

fill my nostrils with spilled coffee
fill my belly with ashes

& let me grab a passerby
& wasp stingers

give me iron fingers
give me a mirror navel

give me deep pocked skin
give me a nail to the eye

lick metal shards
& pound them deep

again
&
again
&
again

III

fill my casket with grass
& seal it up

fill my head with seeds
& let me grab another

fill my nostrils with spilled coffee
& wasp stingers

fill my belly with ashes
& let me grab a passerby

give me iron fingers
&
again

give me a mirror navel
&
again

give me deep pocked skin
&
again

lick metal shards
& pound them deep

give me a nail to the eye

Just Another Stupid White Woman
(Perspective from a state of disbelief:ie; people are rude)

Yep, that's me
Just another stupid white woman

Call me Karen and step away before
I invade your space

Because, mark my words
I will burst your bubble faster than
A squirrel under the tire of a fast car

Faster than the aneurysm in Uncle Fred's head
Faster than a speeding bullet
Faster than Superman himself

But unlike that All-American comic book superhero
I WILL let a train fall from bridge-buckled tracks

My nails cost me a Benjamin and a half
And I had them done y-e-s-t-e-r-d-a-y

Spell it out and listen close honey
No train is gonna chip this shit
And no superhero is gonna shirk his duty on my shift

I am hosting the HOA B-B-Q and I found
The Perfect Dress to go with these acrylics
And these acrylics match my eyes

So whaddya say baby
Want to push my buttons today?

spoken word & the complexity of modern day sociality

awkward interface
that is the definition
I give to any social interaction
that lasts long enough
for my voice to form
words & heaven forbid
sentences

i practice conversations
in advance for days

replay moments of time
on loop
on loop
on loop

for days

ok—
longer than that

it is not enough
to have an hour-long
*closet discussion

*closet discussion:
a discussion carried on between myself, a full closet, and a *clothes chair

*clothes chair:
a chair on which the clothes that do not win the *closet discussion go tc die

Herald of the gods
A nod to Andre dé Shields, Hadestown, NYC, 2022

Every
move
he
made
was
deliberately
perfect

even his flaws were perfect
& i don't have the eyes of a god

his feet played chess with the stage &
he was winning a well thought out game

& i was invested in each step

& he knew—

he demanded investment

& then he sang—

Orleans and a good cry
tears on a trombone slide
with a side of bass

an old song
for a new audience
& a stage full of gods
& the furies

downstairs in The MET

i dabbled in the idea of fashion
design in the eighties
Me, the fashion-free, throw my
hair in bobby pins or shave it off
completely

–coiffure des sans style

Mohawk & combat boots
Flannel & cords

mismatched Converse
& pink plaid pants

what about a good Mohawk is
ever found in the good book of
fashion *faux pas*

never dis a good Mohawk kids

now I have a membership to
The MET
and I only have to fly
two thousand six hundred &
thirty four miles to enjoy its
benefits–

early admission on Thursdays
and an open door to the
members only lounge

sporting miniature muffins–
continental breakfast for
Lilliputians, and a decent cup of
tea for only $24

never dis a good membership
perk
a quiet lounge makes for good conversation–
upraised pinkies to boot

to bote for all you *Old English*
lovers

I'll get to the point

all of the Coco Chanel in the
world
walking down the runway
svelte & smelling mighty fine
fails in comparison

to a moment uninterrupted in
The MET, members only,
Thursday early hours
Exhibition

In America: A Lexicon of Fashion

ANNE FOGARTY (American,
1919-1980)
Evening ensemble, autumn/
winter 1962-63

Ivory wool tweed and jersey

SUPPLENESS

call me Kleenex and what
phase is the moon in—
there has to be a natural
reason for this unnatural
response to all that is
ivory wool tweed and jersey
emotion

& this memory of sketching
haute couture at fourteen

fish skeleton & hacksaw earrings
at sixteen

where's the runway now
Mohawk girl?

These Cathedral Walls Have Flowers as Ears

Step into Cathedral Brugmansia
Carnival church of neurodivergence
Rest a moment under the shade of bougainvillea and grapevine

Flip through the holy pages of
The American Journal of Psychology
Drink wine pressed by the feet of martyrs
Find peace in words of science under buttresses of botany

Holy books bring blossom and brain together
an evolutionary alcove of
bamboo and long sweet grass
preferred by musicians who play Angel's trumpets as warning

Bow your head
Wait for mist to cover you in morning petal-dew
precipital absolution

Pray a rosary of fleshy pearl succulent pleadings
plucked from fingertips by a bird of paradise in velvet robes
deposited in vacant orifices of ogre ears

Listen as priestesses recite
scripture on the back of a dart frog
Sing a psalm from the DSM V's codes and creeping buttercup
chapter 300.29 verse F40.228 a fear of natural things
brought to light through chant and supination

Join hollyhocks who chortle madrigal dissonance
melody against melody
Augmented chords
snap pizz on an upright bass
carved from the Tree of Life

"Do not eat that which is not yours"
"Beautify yourself and drink the blood of your Savior"
"Oh wretched and loved faithful"
"In Her flesh you will find life"

Sacrament of all
All who are lost
All who seek redemption

Hallowed rows burst forth in
Fragrant hallucinatory folly—
a gift from the Goddess of Eternal Psychosis & Generosity
Remember her multitudes

The hungry
The weak
The cold-hearted droves
& Her gifts

Bergamot & belladonna
Wrapped in the skin of the gods

to teach: enseñar

my husband teased me
about my ability to speak Spanish

"you speak like a kindergartner"

he laughed (which i must admit was cute—even his eyes smiled)

still

i felt as stupid as a river rock
unable to move in any direction

i quit trying to speak in family conversations
instead

when my sisters & their husbands & my husband spoke
i listened

i watched telenovelas
without subtitles

i studied the Good Book
in Spanish
English version
to the side

maybe the word of God
would help me speak

hablo
hablas
habla
hablamos
habláis
hablan

what i really wanted was for someone who knew the words
to teach me
para enseñarme

until i could answer back
wiggle from river sludge
& roll into my own smoothness
suavidad

i used to love to write

i wrote my first poem
at three
according to my mother

i traced sand letters at
a drop leaf table

mother's hand guiding mine
—up and down

we named letters together
...aaa...bbb...ccc...

     i wrote early

my love of words grew
as she
read stacks of books
to me

while i
clipped barrettes
in her hair

fifty-one years later
she can still recite
my favorite book

i grew older &
my love of words
grew too

i wrote
about my first born
& those who
followed

i dabbled in words
between
diapers & park visits

between
being teacher
& student

i graded papers
written by kids

in a fast food
parking lot
in winter

& breathed
carbon monoxide
for months

i became
a race car driver
in a parked minivan

lucky
for
me

twice a day
water rituals
oxygenated my blood

i was saved
by side-stroke
& measured laps

     yet

     one

     day

i opened a book
& it
was
   written

in an alien
  lan
    gu
        ag   e

billboards became
picture
        books

my neural
        network –
a stop
light

&

after

fourteen
pages
of
negative
test
results

& cliff hanger
conversations
with doctors

i now know
words like
    dyslexia

        aphasia

    & the phrase
lucky to be alive

—now

it takes longer
    to
read—

hurts more

        &

poetry
feels unworldly—abstract

dictionaries
    feel
mis spe l le d

a paginated puzzle
to find words i loved

        i want

to feel words
take shape
        on table

    or desk

but under my fingers –
even tracing
            words

        feels wrong

lunch: with poets

from time to time
i take myself to lunch

ask for a booth
in a quiet corner

water & a slice of lemon
salad—ranch on the side

something about being
a salad priest excites me

baptism by dressing sprinkle
          each bite
                    equally yoked
    with flavor

humans are nice
when i lunch alone

more smiles
unnecessary pity

i make good company
the book by my elbow
acts as a date

today Momaday—
tomorrow i'll meet

Sylvia & discuss
poetry

broken hearts
recipes for disaster

or have a good country chat
with old e.e. &
his
    blue-
         eyed
boy

Drawing by Lynn Michael Ramsey

subway map

instant gratification isn't found on the 2 train

fifty-seven minutes to Brooklyn
fifty-seven minutes to consider

how many rats die on
subway rails

how many people

and the hum
metal on metal
in two-four time

in seven-eight

in four-four

to lull heavy human cargo on its back in popular time
dare we call it common

Oxford sings: lull—
a temporary interval of quiet or lack of activity

a perfect chord
a devil in three
a little bit of New York City
"Ma-ri-a"

those of you with interval training understand

we are not talking the Alps here
i'm talkin' pure West Side Story shit

Lullaby under Broadway
my head dips between stops
Lullaby on Broadway

bug eyed man try to stare me down again and you will wonder why you
failed—
senza attacca

when my laser eyes burn your neural synapse without apology
—try me
i am trying to sleep away injustice between 42nd street
& a bed in Brooklyn

subway music
creak and sing me to sleep
crawl down into the cavern
of human transportation
no longer pidgin

Creole crooner
sing me to sleep

& wash soot from the walls of un-gentrified stops

& leave your mark

Sign your Name
in dripping paint

in dripping blood

bled dry on a fifty-seven minute commute to bed
from the veins of the walking dead
from the mouths of babes

& your mothers
& your fathers
& your sisters
& your brothers

who commute to unaffordable housing & littered gutters

cum filled condoms strewn along come hither roadways

i am angry sleeping
i am angry sleepwalking
bullshit & rhetoric

these knees

i have moved pianos with these knees
carried sisters & neighbors & cousins

& my own babes

—grandchildren

i have climbed mountains in China
& The Great Wall

craters & beaches

rolling hills of home

stairs of castles

i have walked the streets of cities
country roads
paper route neighborhoods
& nursing homes

i have pedaled with these knees
to city pools
roller-rinks
ice cream scooping drug stores
& walked

to school

to school

to school

i have
knelt in prayer
jumped for joy

danced

fallen down
& stood up
for another go

these knees know gravel
& grass

they
know
pain

& the tear of
fabric pulled in two directions
with the grain

of the material

of me

growth

garden weeds grow unapologetically
& i pull them
root to air
to toss as compost

loamy soil
shoveled scoop by scoop
to become beds
for seeds with latin names

& morning glory
climbs trees
yearns
for a closer sun

open me as i climb
it chortles
much like me
when i stop to rest

turn my face up
& drink beams
as i grasp
for a place to root

to reach

i build leaf piles
throw my hands up
catch the sun & moon

toss them deep
jump in—

bathed in moonglow
i contemplate
that leap & my fate

arms spread wide
i sing—

beams of sun
reach & pull me
deep into the pile

i laugh
& rest

coda

i appreciate a repeat
—a second ending

a moment of
thoughtfulness
in the midst of
an old song

&

time

to reminisce
before the
coda

return home

rolling hills
call me home

velvet blanket
of clay & grass

winter wheat wakes
from quilted slumber

ancient glacial loess
& a fiddle tune

embrace me home

love in a mirror

I wake up
every
single
morning

(on nights I actually sleep)

drag myself to the bathroom
& drop my clothes
on
            the
    floor

look in the mirror
& lean in–

run my fingers over a scar
on my cheek

chant 'I am beautiful"
'I am smart'
'I am capable'
'I am deserving
of
my
love'

solitary redemption

in the erasure
a clearing

(a)new space to discover

i emerge from the ground
earthen womb of women before me
whose shoulders no longer
bear the weight i have released

in the erasure
a breath

(a)new me emerges from the water

free from chains
free from the box
within a box
within a box

And I dance
And I sing
And I feel the sun on my face
And the wind in my hair

(I am) free from chains
I emerge from warmth
surrounded by heartbeat and swoosh
by my mother's heart hymn

I am me
a beginning

I bear scars of gold and silver
trace me beautiful

Dedicated to my beloved companions.
I miss you every single day.

Candy

Our parting well attended

I said goodbye at the feet of an

Angel in Central Park

Spencer
Torado
Eyebrows

Drawing by Lynn Michael Ramsey

About the Author

Cherice Cameron, a native Idahoan, is a mother, writer, artist, and musician whose creative spirit thrives on exploration and discovery. Her travels around the world have instilled in her a deep appreciation for the beauty and solace of nature which serve as a sanctuary and source of inspiration. This eclectic collection of poems, her first foray into published poetry, is a testament to her multifaceted resilience and love of life.

Publisher's Note

Daxson publishing was created to help marginalized artists publish their work, so the world can hear their voice. The vision for this publishing house is to help people get their work out there, and not have them struggle finding their way through the publishing process. Everyone's voice deserves to be heard, and we are here to help. If you are interested in submitting a manuscript, email daxsonpublishing@gmail.com.

www.ingramcontent.com/pod-product-compliance
Lightning Source LLC
Chambersburg PA
CBHW020420130626
46549CB00006B/2661